the challenge of
change
leadership strategies for
not-for-profit executives and boards

by philip coltoff

The Challenge of Change
Leadership Strategies for
Not-for-Profit Executives and Boards

This book was published
and printed thanks to the support of the
JPMorganChase Foundation
and the
New York University School of Social Work
in cooperation with
The Children's Aid Society.

Book design by Hans Callenbach Design

Philip Coltoff
Library of Congress Control Number: 2006932828
Copyright © 2006 by Philip Coltoff
Published in 2006

Printed in the United States

ISBN 978-0-9788903-0-8
ISBN 0-9788903-0-2

13 12 11 10 09 08 07 06   1 2 3 4 5

www.childrensaidsociety.org

The Challenge of Change

Leadership Strategies for
Not-for-Profit Executives and Boards

By Philip Coltoff

To my children—Michael, Robert, Julie, Peter, and the most recent additions, Megan and Rachel. To all of my seven grandchildren. And to the thousands of children who over the years have crossed my path.

Contents

1. Core Values

2. The Key Issues

3. Lessons in Leadership

Acknowledgments

There are so many people who deserve my thanks that I cannot possibly identify them all. First, I must thank my wife, Lynn, who has been a great source of encouragement, a motivator, and, at times, a constructive provocateur. I am also deeply grateful to the board of trustees and officers of The Children's Aid Society, who have provided me with the opportunity not only to direct this incredible organization but also to write about it. I cannot offer enough thanks to my administrative assistant, Angela Pelliccia, who suffered with me through the long, trying hours of putting this book together. Appreciation is also due to my in-house editor, the talented, ever-watchful fact-checker, detailer, and idea maker, Lisa Glazer, and to my expert copy editor, Mark Sorkin. It was also a pleasure working with book designer Hans Callenbach. I am indebted to scores of peers who have reviewed the many drafts and made constructive suggestions, never hurtful, always helpful. My sincere thanks to a special group of colleagues and friends:

Eric Brettschneider

Dr. Michael A. Carrera

Jan Correa

Dr. Sidney Harman

Daniel Kronenfeld

Allan Luks

Kathleen Clark Moses

Jane Quinn

Dr. Gary Rosenberg

Jack Rosenthal

Michael Stoller

Neil Waldman

Finally, I extend heartfelt thanks to Suzanne England, professor and dean of the New York University School of Social Work; Judy Dimon, The Children's

Aid Society trustee and confidante; and Kimberly Davis, president of the JPMorganChase Foundation. I am thankful that with their help and assistance, this book will see the light of day.

Foreword

When an early version of Philip Coltoff's book, *The Challenge of Change*, landed on my desk, I was surprised to find that our philosophies on leadership are amazingly consistent despite (minor) generational differences. Most important, Phil affirmed my core belief that not-for-profit leadership requires a conscious blend of "the head and the heart."

As president of the JPMorganChase Foundation, coming from a business background with a keen passion for community, I was excited to finally read a leadership guide *by* a not-for-profit executive *for* not-for-profit executives. I found Phil's book so powerful and so practical that I offered to support its publication, bringing his ideas to not-for-profit program managers, officers, and leaders around the country.

Times are changing, and this book provides a useful guide. Not-for-profit leadership requires a keen understanding of the motivations and expectations of all of its constituents, particularly corporate funders. Funders expect—no, *demand*—not-for-profit leaders to be constantly developing new and breakthrough ways to solve old problems. Phil offers many solutions and he challenges leaders to balance courage, focus, and drive with passion, compassion, and inspiration.

His discussion on the "new era of accountability" in this time of high expectations and complete transparency was music to my ears. As funders continue to make difficult choices and trade-offs in evaluating who and where to fund, Phil's instruction to the not-for-profit leader is clear and simple: be ready to prove and defend the impact of your programs. Yet Phil also advises funders to recognize that solely quantifiable measures are not the only way to measure success. Excellent advice.

I count Phil Coltoff as a friend and mentor. I thank him for sharing his leadership lessons with the world. His book affirms the notion that leadership skills are transferable. Whether you're in the not-for-profit or for-profit field, either way you can learn from Phil's wisdom.

Kimberly Davis

President

JPMorganChase Foundation

Preface

Ｉt is my great good fortune to know Phil Coltoff, and I am further blessed by the fact that he is now executive-in-residence and the Katherine and Howard Aibel Visiting Professor at the New York University School of Social Work, where I consult with him on an almost daily basis. As dean of the School of Social Work, I have ready access to one of the best minds (and most generous hearts) in not-for-profit leadership today. Talk about executive coaching!

When Phil gave me a draft of this book and I saw how small it was, I confess I was a bit skeptical. Being accustomed to the tomes on management and leadership that fill the shelves of my bookcase, I wondered how this slim volume (by a real live executive, no less, and not a Harvard Business School professor) could possibly communicate the breadth and depth of his experience. I could talk with Phil for hours on end and still only begin to scratch the surface of his wisdom. How could this small book capture the essence of that wisdom and offer practical advice as well?

Even after several readings, I still can't say for sure how he does it, but somehow Phil chooses just the right topic or example to hone in like a laser on the core issues facing executives and boards. Reading this book was so much like sitting down for a conversation with Phil that I could actually hear his voice and was constantly reminded of how well he listens—a testament to a writer who cares deeply about his reader.

I found this book to be not only inspiring but liberating. Phil speaks plain truths that are seldom voiced and is not afraid to tell of his own struggles and of how much he has learned and gained from others. For all of its practicality and wisdom, what makes this book stand apart is its unwavering attention to moral principles. Executives and board members are by definition very smart and highly skilled at what they do, but as we so sadly know, it is the failure of moral reasoning that can compromise and even destroy a movement or an organization. As Phil demonstrates in his examples and advice, this is the true bottom line.

In his many years of service and now in this book, Phil Coltoff exemplifies the servant leader. In the words of Dr. Martin Luther King Jr., "Anyone can serve.... You only need to have a heart full of grace. A soul generated by Love."

Suzanne England

Professor and Dean

New York University School of Social Work

Introduction

"If it ain't broke, don't fix it." I don't know who said that first. Benjamin Franklin? Yogi Berra? In any case, in my eighteen years as trustee and twelve years as president and now chairman of the board of The Children's Aid Society, it has been my guiding principle. You see, I've been tremendously fortunate to have Philip Coltoff as the organization's leader. Because of that, I had the easiest job in the world.

Phil's leadership was tireless, always right-on, and—this is so rare—he combined superb attention to detail with inspiring vision. Oh, he kept me and the board fully informed and often asked for advice. However, in his nearly twenty-five years at the helm, it was Phil more than anyone else who increased our budget from $10 million to $80 million; it was Phil more than anyone else who increased the number of children we serve from 80,000 to almost twice that number; it was Phil more than anyone else who made The Children's Aid Society the great organization it is today. The French philosopher Voltaire once said, "The best is the enemy of the good." Well, in that sense, Phil was always the enemy of the good; he always went for the best—and achieved the best.

Now retired from the CEO position, Phil has become a special adviser to Children's Aid. In this excellent book, he extends his advice beyond the organization, drawing upon the experience of his years as our executive director and CEO and drawing from them guidance for other not-for-profit leaders, both current and prospective. I have seen the lessons he offers in practice—and believe me, they work.

I know that in saying this, I echo the views of my predecessors who also had Phil as their CEO— John Griswold, Charlton Phelps, Edward Lamont, and Nicholas Scoppetta—as well as those of our current president, Dr. Angela Diaz. We have all benefited greatly from Phil's knowledge and expertise and are confident that you, the reader, will do so as well.

Edgar R. Koerner

Chairman of the Board

The Children's Aid Society

CHAPTER 1
Core Values

Staying True to the Not-for-Profit Ideal

This book is brief for a reason: I don't want it to sit on your bedside table with all the other professional literature waiting for your attention. Instead, I'm hoping you will pick it up, stay with it from start to finish, and absorb it in a few quick hours.

My purpose is to distill the insights I've gained from nearly twenty-five years of leadership at The Children's Aid Society of New York City, one of the largest and best-known not-for-profit organizations in the nation, and to share my ideas and experiences with a new generation of not-for-profit leaders and board members.

Our sector has grown exponentially in recent decades—and so has the responsibility of its leaders. This book offers useful tools to respond to changing times:

1

new government demands, new accountability mea-sures, new expectations from funders. It also provides my perspective on timeless issues, like how best to lead your staff and how to handle crises. Much has been written about the role of today's executive, but most of it is dry and theoretical. My goal is to offer dynamic, practical, easy-to-read advice, not only for current ex-ecutive directors but also for mid-level managers who aspire to become directors.

Throughout this book, you will find some recur-ring themes: the need for strong and secure leadership, the importance of taking thoughtful risks and standing up for principles, the value of respect in all interactions, and the merits of pushing yourself and others toward excellence. I also stress repeatedly that we need to re-main true to the ideals of social change, of making life better for those in need, even when these ideals are out of sync with our materialistic, winner-take-all society.

Today's not-for-profit is structurally much more similar to corporate America than it has been at any time in the past. We are charitable but cost-conscious, dedicated to helping people, and mission-driven. Our organizational systems often rely on corporate models, and we market our services, use the media, recruit staff, raise money, and sometimes even lobby the government along corporate lines.

Elements of corporate style are certainly useful for not-for-profits. But we should never apply a corporate vision to the substance of our work. Our purpose is improving the lives of society's most vulnerable citizens, a slow and difficult but vitally important process that requires long-range vision and commitment, not a short-term focus on cost-benefit ratios. Although we can chart our achievements by tallying graduation and employment rates or calculating the dollars saved by preventing teen pregnancy or youth incarceration, our most important results are more personal—and more profound. I think of Kanema, a young cellist from one of our community schools in Washington Heights who got her start in our string orchestra and is winning scholarships and tutoring young musicians at the age of fifteen. As she puts it, "I now know anything is possible."

My understanding of the importance of this sense of possibility has been shaped by both my personal and professional background. I was raised in the Bronx in a working-class family, and I earned my undergraduate degree at the City College of New York. I chose to work in the not-for-profit world not only because I wanted to make an impact on the poverty and inequality all around me but also because my identity was influenced by my positive experiences at the Freeman Street Y in the South Bronx and as a youth worker for the Williamsburg Y in Brooklyn.

At seventeen, I worked as a counselor at the Freeman Street Y's Ella Fohs Camp, leading a diverse group of children from very poor backgrounds and loving every minute of it. The camp was run by social workers, and they treated me so respectfully, giving me the same in-depth direction and supervision they provided to college students and young professionals, that my own sense of self grew enormously. I was entirely satisfied by my summer earnings ($50, which went a long way in 1953), but when I was told at the end of the season that I was the only youth counselor to receive a bonus of an additional $50—well, at that point I knew I'd found my calling.

Before completing my master's degree in social work at New York University, I took a job as the teen director at the Williamsburg Y through a program run by the New York City Youth Board. Think *West Side Story* to get a sense of the time. The neighborhood was overrun by gangs wielding knives and zip guns, a type of homemade pistol; my job was reaching out to Puerto Rican, Italian, and Jewish street kids and introducing them to the Y. I tried to create a sphere of safety, urging troubled teens to join team sports and groups addressing the tough issues affecting their lives. With attention and support, many turned away from violence. I'm still in touch with some of them today.

After a number of years working in youth-serving and mental-health agencies and a short stint researching youth crime and delinquency for a national policy group, I joined The Children's Aid Society in 1966 as program director. I have stayed here ever since, serving in positions of steadily increasing responsibility: assistant director, associate director, executive director, and CEO. I recently stepped down from the executive position and now serve as a special adviser and consultant to the agency. I have also had the distinction of being appointed executive-in-residence and visiting professor at New York University's School of Social Work.

Working for Children's Aid was and remains an immense honor and responsibility. The organization was founded in 1853 by Charles Loring Brace, a reform-minded minister committed to improving the living conditions and life opportunities of New York City's street children. Brace was prodigiously driven, and within his lifetime he created a vast network of lodging houses for homeless boys and girls, as well as industrial schools that taught skills like cobbling and hand-sewing, and the "orphan trains" that sent thousands of poor and abandoned city children to live with families in rural America.

Over the years, Children's Aid has become renowned as an agency of "firsts"—we created the nation's first free lunch program, the city's first free dental clinics, the state's first mediation service diverting youth from family court. Many of our programs and services, past and present, have led to paradigm shifts in social services: from the orphan trains, which laid the groundwork for modern foster care, to our full-service community schools, which offer a new vision for public education.

The scope of our work today is far-reaching. With an annual budget of about $80 million, our services touch the lives of 150,000 children and families, mostly in low-income New York City communities like Central Harlem, Washington Heights, the South Bronx, and Bedford-Stuyvesant in Brooklyn. Our programs and services include early-childhood education; winter and summer camps; Boys & Girls Clubs; community centers; community schools; foster care and adoption; medical, dental, and mental-health clinics; teen pregnancy prevention; youth mentoring; and performing and visual arts.

Most of our work involves direct services, but we are also advocates and innovators with an active role in the national debate about children's health, education, and welfare. I am especially proud of our teen-pregnancy-prevention and community schools programs, which have a combined total of nearly 1,600 replication and adaptation sites nationally and internationally.

This description should not give the impression that this book is only suitable for people who run large not-for-profits. Far from it. Even if I repeatedly give examples from Children's Aid, my goal is to address issues that are central to all social-service and youth-development organizations, regardless of size. While writing, I remembered a book by Rudolph Wittenberg,

So You Want to Help People, which guided me at the beginning of my career. Wittenberg's book was a bible for youth workers of my era, reprinted four times and then reissued in a condensed format as part of the Leadership Library series. My dog-eared original copy has pencil underlines and annotations in the margin, and I still keep it close by in my office.

I hope this book will be equally useful, and I welcome your comments, feedback, and suggestions. As H.L. Mencken once said, "There is always a well-known solution to every human problem—neat, plausible, and wrong." I trust that my observations will be neat and plausible. I don't rule out that some may indeed be wrong... but I hope not.

Careful readers will notice that I alternate use of personal pronouns; if I refer to the director as "he" in one chapter, I use "she" in the next. In so doing, my goal is to ensure the book resonates with all readers, male and female. I also refer to the leaders of not-for-profit organizations using a number of terms: director, executive director, chief executive officer. I use them interchangeably and they all mean the same thing: the professional in charge.

Key Points

- As the not-for-profit sector has grown, so has the responsibility of its leaders.

- Many not-for-profit organizations today have structural similarities to for-profit corporations.

- Nonetheless, not-for-profits should steer clear of a corporate vision and remain focused on improving the lives of society's most vulnerable citizens.

CHAPTER 2

The Key Issues

Working with the Board: Twenty-First-Century Strategies

When I first joined The Children's Aid Society some forty years ago, I discovered that several of our trustees were the second and third generation within their families to serve on our board. They regaled me with stories of our nineteenth-century board members, almost all male and Episcopalian, from the leading families of the time. Board meetings were held most often at the Harvard Club, with board members in black tie. I often imagine them reclining in leather armchairs in front of a roaring fire, sipping brandy and smoking cigars, earnestly conferring on how best to serve the city's children.

Our board today is very different, yet our concerns about children remain the same. We now include men and women, young and old, white and black, Latina and Latino, Christian and Jewish. Our roster still includes prominent and well-to-do members of New York society, but we also have many male and female leaders from the communities and constituents we serve. Their ranks include an entrepreneur from Harlem, a doctor born in the Dominican Republic and raised in Washington Heights, and an African-American state Supreme Court Justice who created a mentoring program for at-risk youth in Brooklyn.

This diversity, which reflects our urban environment, represents The Children's Aid Society today and tomorrow—and the future for most not-for-profit youth-serving organizations nationwide. Yet even as board membership is changing, in many instances relationships between the board and the staff reflect an earlier era. This issue—whether an organization is board-driven or staff-driven—is of central importance and merits full discussion. Let's start with some historical background.

The first not-for-profits were established in the early to mid-1800s in the United States to help the disabled, the handicapped, the hospitalized, the needy, and children. Their approach was an outgrowth of the Elizabethan Poor Laws of 1601, which required the aristocracy to serve the "deserving poor." Wealthy families founded and ran these organizations, which reached out to the "halt and the lame" and became known from then until now as charities.

The earliest charities included not only The Children's Aid Society but also the Charity Organization Society of America, the Society for Improving the Condition of the Poor, the City Mission Society, Community Service Society, Catholic Foundling, and, a few decades later, the Boys Clubs of America. This was also the time of the first hospitals and settlement houses: places like Hull House in Chicago, Bellevue Hospital in New York City, and University Settlement on the Lower East Side. These institutions were known as "voluntary" because volunteers ran them. They helped poor immigrant children and families on practical matters including literacy, socialization, and basic sanitation. The government provided almost no support to these institutions and did not get into the business of helping charities until the Great Depression.

The role of the volunteers began to change and diminish in the first half of the twentieth century, as social work schools opened their doors and the social sciences became more established, leading charities to hire paid staff with a more comprehensive view of human behavior. This movement was greatly influenced by the emergence of Freudian psychology, the beliefs of social workers such as Jane Addams, and the modern theories of education espoused by John Dewey, Maria Montessori, and Jean Piaget. The paid staff were referred to as head workers, counselors, agents, or social workers. Many were part of President Franklin Delano Roosevelt's New Deal, and they were doing good: they earned little but felt accomplished and, at times, even pure of heart.

As professionals moved into charities, the founders—the volunteers—often worked with them side-by-side. The volunteers ran the organizations and later constituted a board of directors or trustees. The professionals were few and far between; while respected and needed, they were seen as hired help, and they responded to the volunteers in ways that were typical of most domestic relationships.

In general, one was rich and the other was poor or working-class. One was the boss and the other was subordinate. While I am simplifying this relationship, the culture that grew out of this relationship was influential for many years. Even as not-for-profit organizations grew in size and became more professional, in many instances the relationship between the trustees and the paid staff, including the executive director, didn't fundamentally change. The executive director was nominally in charge, but he or she did not truly guide the organization's mission and direction. This inherent inequality had a considerable impact, defining roles and functions for decades to follow.

Executive directors often deferred to board members when they could have or should have had input into decision-making. Many executives believed that the board was omniscient and did not trust their own professional judgments or feared the consequences of making even the right decisions. They behaved as subordinates, and this behavior, coupled with the perception that they were less qualified, often did not allow real professional growth or essential change.

This pattern of stalled evolution was not the same for large medical institutions and universities. Because of the nature of their work, their mission, and high level of expertise, the trustees of these organizations have largely deferred important issues to the professionals. In universities, boards seldom interfere with the teaching curricula or the free expression of the scholars within. In hospitals, the trustees defer to the medical experts and health professionals for the delivery and evaluation of services.

In the world of social-service and youth-serving organizations, however, things developed differently. Board members often did not differentiate themselves in knowledge, skill, and competence from the professionals. This is partly because psychology, social work, recreation therapy, and counseling were not as highly esteemed as medicine or pure academics. It is also because the volunteers in social-service organizations were so "hands on." Day in and day out, they worked in community centers and settlement houses, tutoring, mentoring, educating, even visiting the clients at home. They ran the organizations, did the work, and received the satisfaction of working directly with children and families in need.

As times have changed, so has the relationship between the board and the professionals. Ever so gradually, board members who are investment bankers, business leaders, attorneys, and advertising executives have come to recognize the value of professionals whose knowledge and expertise in this field are greater than their own. The change also reflects broader changes in society. Even the wealthiest individuals, women as well as men, are today less inclined to volunteer on a daily basis and more likely to find paid employment. There is simply less time to spend in the settlement house, Boys & Girls Club, or recreation center.

However, the perception of the board with respect to the chief executive is another matter. Even if the board now understands that staff members have special skills for dealing with clients, recognition of the executive's leadership and managerial skills often remains an issue of concern.

History is important because the pull and tug over power and decision-making still exists, although change is occurring. Some board members from the business world still desire the upper hand, believing they are better equipped with management skills. Yet at the same time, the executive who was trained in the social sciences and has worked directly with children and families may also have acquired the requisite managerial skills. He now believes that he is in the best position to make the important decisions with respect to personnel; budgeting; relationships with foundation, corporate, and government officials; and evaluating the agency's performance.

Like most things, the issue of direction and leadership has many twists and turns. Unfortunately, some board members hold tight reins over their executive directors and limit their ability to exercise their rightful functions. It's a control issue. Equally unfortunate, many not-for-profit executives voluntarily relinquish their authority and yield to the board president, chairman, or committee head. Discussion and consensus-building between the board and an executive are fine, but the final decision-making should not reside solely with the board. When an executive director feels insecure and threatened or intimidated and worried about keeping his job, he compromises not only his own position as leader but his staff's ability to function with the needed autonomy and independence that all professionals should enjoy. Fortunately, this was not the case at Children's Aid, where the relationship between the board and the CEO was close, sharing, and affectionate but respectful of the proper boundaries.

To be sure, board members have a most important place in the governance of the agency. They provide continuity while executive directors may come and go. They hire the director and evaluate his performance, ideally on an annual basis. The board and its officers have fiduciary responsibility and ultimately are the ones who must defend the agency's practices, accomplishments, or failures. Nonetheless, upholding this responsibility does not mean overstepping boundaries and crossing into the professional arena. When it does occur, it reduces the board's own effectiveness as well as the agency's capacity to deliver its services.

Executive directors who continuously struggle with an old-fashioned and overbearing board need to think strategically about how to foster change. Useful steps include introducing new board members from the communities being served, which adds essential new voices to decision-making and helps organizations meet government requirements for an integrated and diverse governing body. Another approach is to develop an advisory council made up of volunteers and younger people drawn from all walks of life. The advisory council should be seen as a training ground for the board, with members attending board and committee meetings and given meaningful responsibilities that enable new leadership to shine. These steps take considerable time, attention, and effort, but they will bring the board into contemporary times.

The best boards function cohesively, with a spirit of shared goals and interests, but in these busy times it is difficult to build bonds among board members. At The Children's Aid Society, we invite board members to attend an annual educational trip to review child welfare programs in other countries, usually at the invitation of foreign governments. Attendance is voluntary, and board members pay for their own trip; those

who have attended say the experience has strength-
ened their ties to other board members and their con-
nection to Children's Aid.

Process Versus Progress: The Age of Evaluation

Like the eternal question about which came first, the
chicken or the egg, the not-for-profit world is torn
between process and progress. While not-for-profits
have historically been concerned with the "process" of
change, it has become increasingly important to quantify our "progress." This is one of the most significant
changes I've observed over the course of my career.

It wasn't always this way. In my early working years,
it was implicitly understood that our work involved
changes that occur to people over a period of time,
and it was sufficient to report on the ongoing effects
of an intervention for abused children, teens placed in
a group home, or victims of domestic violence. We all
recognize that change builds upon itself, allowing indi-

viduals to grow over time. We know that this progression can be self-directed or directed by others. While very hard to measure, it is crucial for human development and growth.

Yet the "process" approach has come under considerable scrutiny in the past ten years. Many people now believe it permits a wishy-washy sequence of events with no end in sight. Indeed, social work has often been accused of using an emphasis on "process" to avoid the challenge of providing hard evidence of success or failure for a given intervention, program, or strategy.

In response, foundation boards and government agencies are increasingly requiring an approach borrowed from the worlds of medicine and business: fact-finding, diagnosis, prescription, treatment, and evaluation. In many instances, social agencies have found creative ways of adapting to this expectation and presenting identifiable outcomes that withstand review. Even something as seemingly unquantifiable as a child's level of self-esteem can be measured, to some degree, through carefully designed self-reporting by program participants.

During my leadership, The Children's Aid Society published many in-depth evaluations—some conducted in-house, others researched and written by university experts—and the vast majority showed the profound impact of our programs through clear indicators and outcomes. Yet I also saw that the most important work can also be the most difficult to quantify. We need to be aware of this and resist the push to either rapidly achieve overly ambitious outcomes or focus our evaluations only on outcomes that are simple to measure.

I learned this lesson firsthand from the challenges that emerged from evaluations of our work with children, families, and institutions with long and complex histories—teens "aging out" of foster care, homeless families, and overwhelmed public schools.

Our work within public schools, in particular, is

instructive. Let me start by describing our community schools program, one of our best. Based on a simple premise, that learning does not occur in isolation from the rest of a child's life, our program brings the services children need to grow, develop, and learn directly into their schools. These services include not only after-school programs but also on-site medical, dental, and mental health-care as well as Family Resource Centers, Saturday programs, and summer camps. Working in partnership with New York City's Department of Education, The Children's Aid Society currently operates fifteen community schools, and our program model has been adapted in about 1,500 sites nationally and internationally.

Our schools truly offer the opportunity for transformation, and I see this every time I meet with parents in the communities we serve. I vividly recall, in particular, sitting in on a focus group facilitated by the Ad Council when they were developing a national promotional campaign for community schools. This session, which was led in English and Spanish by a highly skilled fa-cilitator, brought together fourteen community school parents, all of them immigrants, most of whom had been in the country less than five years. One parent described in Spanish how her middle-school child had seen a dentist for the first time in our clinic and had a whole mouth of cavities filled. Another spoke about how her child had attempted suicide several times but had received extensive support from our social work-ers and was finally doing well. A third emphasized how our after-school programs made it possible for her to work, knowing her child was in a safe environment until 7 p.m. To my surprise, only three of the parents understood that The Children's Aid Society was pro-viding these services, but that was least important to the parents. What I took away from that day was their belief that our services should be available not only in their school but in all schools.

Turning this vision into a realistic expansion plan required hard data, and from the very beginning of our community schools program we understood the importance of evaluation. Early studies by researchers from Fordham University in the 1990s examined our first New York City community schools in relation to comparison schools and found promising evidence of school-wide improvements in test scores and numerous other positive results, including less school violence, higher student attendance, greater parent involvement, and improvements in the overall school climate. The most consistent comment the researchers heard from staff and families was that the wealth of services provided by Children's Aid freed teachers to focus on teaching. These exciting findings helped us make the case for rapid growth.

As we sought to make an impact on the national education agenda, we knew we needed other evaluations to track improvements over time. Funders wanted this, the public wanted this, *we* wanted this. But then things got complicated. In some of our community schools, scores stabilized or fell as educators implemented new standardized tests and teachers and students struggled to meet higher expectations.

I continued to push for an evaluation that linked our progress to test scores. Yet I kept remembering the advice of Lisbeth Schorr, a lecturer in social medicine at Harvard University, who suggested early on that clear-cut academic improvements might be beyond our reach in the near term and counseled us to focus instead on children's physical, social, and emotional gains. The facts have proven her right. Despite our fourteen-year partnership with the Department of Education, there is so much we can't control—the Byzantine politics of the school system, the quality of the school-day teachers, student mobility, principal turnover, the content of the school-day curriculum, the challenges of teaching large numbers of special-ed students and even larger numbers of students learning English as a second language. At this point in time, it's hard to prove a consistent, school-wide impact on test scores, even as we see a continuing pattern of strong outcomes in other important indicators, especially mental and physical health and reductions in special-education referrals.

The mixed results on test scores do not mean that we should abandon our efforts—just the opposite. Across the country, the single-minded focus on standardized testing makes our after-school programs and support services, with their focus on developing the whole child, more important than ever. Thanks to the leadership of our National Technical Assistance Center for Community Schools and our active collaboration with other community organizations and educational advocacy groups in the United States and overseas, our model continues to expand to scale.

The results from our most recent evaluation by ActKnowledge, Inc., an independent research firm based at the Graduate Center of the City University of New York, are encouraging. They show that students who participated in after-school programs at community schools improved their academics significantly more than students who did not participate— and that the gap between the two groups widened as the length of student participation in our programs increased. As we keep evaluating our outcomes, I'm cautiously optimistic that this pattern of positive results will continue.

Systemic change requires a quality we like to call "stick-to-it-iveness." In our community schools program, this has meant accepting the limits of social science research and rising to the challenge of the real world in which we work. Our assistant executive director for community schools, Jane Quinn, along with Joy G. Dryfoos and Carol Barkin, recently edited *Community Schools in Action: Lessons from a Decade of Practice*; in the concluding chapter they offer three mantras guiding the core operation of community schools:

- It's all about relationships.
- Everything has to be negotiated, all the time.
- To make partnerships work, you have to have the word "yes" written in your heart.

In other words, pay attention to process—and the progress will come.

Strategic Planning: Guidelines, Not God Lines

Another significant change in recent decades has been the rise in prominence of strategic planning. While this process is useful, we need to resist the push to plan as though we are General Motors or Dell.

We are not in the business of producing more cars or computers. Instead, we are working with complex human beings, people who are struggling to reduce dependency on alcohol or drugs, families who are attempting to achieve stability, children who are learning to love and trust adults after years of abuse. Our strategic plans should reflect this reality, focusing on strategies to influence positive changes in people's lives.

After gathering input, the executive director and senior staff members should shape the strategic plan. Board members should be informed and at times be

active participants in the process. The executive director should resist the inclination of some board members, who may insist on developing a strategic plan
along the business model, which isn't oriented toward
change outcomes. A not-for-profit strategic plan is as
much interpretive as it is descriptive, and there should
always be opportunities for change and modifications.
All too often I have heard not-for-profit executives
speak of the strategic plan as a "god line" rather than a
guideline. These executives end up twisting facts to fit
the requirements of the plan. This becomes a terrible
waste of time and effort, turning the entire process into
a sham.

Strategic planning can take many shapes and forms.
One approach involves charting the direction of a not-
for-profit and deciding where best to focus attention
and resources. We underwent this process at The Children's Aid Society about ten years ago, spurred by a
report by the Carnegie Council on Adolescent Development, *A Matter of Time: Risk and Opportunities in the*

Non-School Hours, revealing that most youth-serving organizations had a dearth of programs for teens. After an internal assessment, we found that our support for younger children was much stronger than our support for teens, and we resolved to do more. Instead of instantly creating a raft of new programs, we started with research. How many teens were we serving? How many more could we accommodate in our facilities? What could we learn about their age, gender, socioeconomic status, and educational aspirations?

We took an inventory of other agencies in our communities and ultimately saw a wide gap in services, which led us to develop new priorities for programs and services. It took a few years, but over time we expanded our sports, college scholarship, teen pregnancy prevention, and employment internship programs. Later on, we created the Hope Leadership Academy and implemented a comprehensive new support program for the young people returning home from juvenile detention facilities. We recognized that teens need to play a major role in the development and leadership of their programs; this understanding shaped the Hope Leadership Academy, which trains teens in leadership skills and conflict resolution. Because of our strategic planning process, teen participation has increased exponentially throughout our program sites.

Another strategic planning approach involves reviewing and revising all services and programs to ensure they are on a path of continuous improvement. We underwent this process about five years ago at The Children's Aid Society, relying on departmental leaders and their staff to develop key outcome indicators for their work. Each service area—foster care, community centers, camps, health and dental, community schools, and so forth—created its own plan, and then the various plans were merged into a larger agency document. Outcomes meetings were held regularly with staff from each of the major service areas. We didn't include support services such as fundraising, public relations, or human resources, but in retrospect we should have.

This approach to strategic planning led to better collective thinking and quicker corrective changes, particularly at our uptown health clinic, a beautiful medical and dental facility within our popular Dunlevy Milbank community center in Central Harlem. The urgent and unmet health needs of Harlem's residents are well known—one 1990 study in *The New England Journal of Medicine* famously revealed that African-American males in Harlem were less likely to reach age sixty-five than males in Bangladesh. So we expected that after a long-awaited renovation, our facility would be very busy, serving at least 100 patients a day, but month after month the clinic was struggling to meet this goal.

When we addressed this issue at outcomes meetings, the staff were initially defensive, blaming the problem on colleagues who were supposed to refer children from the extensive after-school program for annual physical and dental reviews. Another issue was the subsequent establishment of numerous competing health facilities in the community. How could we overcome these barriers? The staff's defensiveness dissipated when the whole team started to explore proactive solutions.

We decided to spend time on outreach, meeting one-on-one not only with parents who sent their children to our after-school program but also with the families in our nearby homeless shelter, day-care center, and Carmel Hill community support program.

We solved the problem by thinking creatively, reaching out to our community, and working together: within a few months, the clinic was meeting its service goal. This change was the result of sound strategic planning, a process that included both flexibility and accountability.

The New Accountability

After a decade of corporate and not-for-profit scandals—not only at Enron and WorldCom but also at the United Way and the American Red Cross—we're in a new era of accountability, a time of high expectations and potentially harsh penalties. Listen up!

Not-for-profit executives are accountable on many levels to many constituencies: to their boards, funding sources, government agencies, and the general public. They report through the agency's annual reports, financial statements, and audits. The agency's financial statements and audits should be comprehensive, attested to by independent auditors, and clearly signed off by the executive director and chief financial officer. They should be readily available to the public, ideally on a website, ensuring easy access for all and complete transparency.

Programmatic accountability is equally important and needs a structure, whether it is regular outcome reviews, clear performance standards, or regular evaluations (either internal or independent). All constituent players should be informed on a continuous and regular basis of the efficacy of the agency and its programmatic integrity. How is this done? At The Children's

Aid Society, we try to provide program updates to donors and funders at least twice a year. We also publish a
newsletter, numerous reports and publications, and our
website is updated regularly. While we always empha-
size our progress, we also acknowledge setbacks and
failures. This type of reporting helps an agency develop
and maintain a reputation for integrity.

We also spend considerable time reporting to the
government, responding to new and tougher performance standards and ever-more-stringent rules for
contracting. These changes are legitimate, even if elements of the reporting process are onerous and at times
seem counterproductive. While we may not always
agree with government accountability performance
standards—and we should try to convince government
agencies to be more realistic—we nevertheless need to
make every effort to do well on those standards and to
outperform the averages. When we do, we gain additional credibility with funders and the public.

Another important shift is the Sarbanes–Oxley Act

of 2002, which requires a demanding new level of corporate reporting and accountability. Most of this influential legislation, passed following corporate accounting debacles, is not yet applicable to the not-for-profit world—but it may be soon. Across the country, legislators are exploring ways to extend its provisions to our realm.

There are many useful provisions within Sarbanes-Oxley: a board executive committee, an executive compensation committee, an audit committee with independent members, a staff code of conduct, a whistle-blower provision, and an annual conflict-of-interest statement signed by trustees, specifically referring to self-dealing. Many mature not-for-profits already have these provisions in place; all not-for-profit agencies, large and small, should be proactive and implement these measures.

The real concern, however, involves board liability. Currently, board members of not-for-profit organizations are not personally responsible if their executive director makes unethical or illegal decisions (although there has been at least one court decision to the contrary). Some of the more recently proposed legislation at both the federal and local levels includes liability and penalties to board members for acts of omission, not just commission. This is obviously a cause for concern, and even alarm, not only among board members but also executives.

Executive directors who prefer to remain silent about key agency issues and problems need to change their habits so that board members are not left exposed and vulnerable.

It is essential to inform board members about the coverage and limits of directors' and officers' insurance. There should be open disclosure with respect to all major decisions, particularly those pertaining to significant donations, big-ticket expenditures, and anything that could be interpreted by others as a sweetheart deal or self-dealing. If you're starting a major renovation, seek bids from multiple contractors and choose the best company at the best price, avoiding special deals with companies owned or controlled by a board member. If a major donation comes in earmarked for a specific program, keep it in a restricted account and don't use it for other purposes, even when finances are tight. It's better to take out a short-term loan to meet cash flow needs than violate the terms of a grant agreement. If you hire a senior staff member who requires unusually high compensation or special allowances for housing or transportation, the board officers need to know the terms of the deal and have an outside firm assess the factors of compensation in the appropriate universe.

Board members should be informed at every available opportunity of accountability issues, even if they don't appear to be especially interested or concerned about this topic. All of this is part of the new governance and accountability. It should be lived with, not feared nor put aside. Those who avoid or ignore it do so at their own peril.

Key Points

- As times have changed, so has the role of board members, particularly regarding decision-making.

- To bring a board into the twenty-first century, recruit new and younger board members from the communities being served. Consider creating an advisory council that is a training ground for the board.

- Today's executive directors need to assert strong leadership and develop equal relationships of mutual respect with the board.

- "Doing good" is no longer good enough. To survive and thrive, not-for-profits need to provide measurable outcomes for their work.

- Nonetheless, some of the most important work is the hardest to quantify. Leaders need to resist the push to achieve overly ambitious results.

- In the not-for-profit world, strategic planning should be a flexible process. It's about charting directions and changing lives, not number crunching.

- Recent legislation has ushered in a new era of

accountability, accompanied by high expectations and potentially harsh penalties.

- In order to maintain compliance with new governmental regulations, executive directors and boards need to place a high priority on transparency.

CHAPTER 3

Lessons in Leadership

Essential Qualities of Leadership

The executive director is the central leader and the prime mover within an organization. She sails the ship and if she exercises her leadership correctly, she will guide the ship not only into calm waters but new oceans.

To succeed, the not-for-profit leader needs to gain the support of her board and her staff and to earn their respect in ways that allow her to exercise her leadership in a forthright manner. If the executive is respectful, direct, honest and strong, she is more likely to have a board that reflects similar qualities. If, on the other hand, she is indecisive and yields or abdicates her authority, she no doubt will have a confused, overbearing, or ineffectual board.

Another measure of a leader is how she establishes

the "culture of the agency." The culture constitutes the mores and values, as well as the written and unwritten rules and regulations of an organization. It includes client focus, sound ethical values, concern for people's well-being, and respect for confidentiality.

The executive director establishes this culture through her own behavior, not through distributed memorandums. Her conduct, style, dress, and conversational tone create the culture that permeates the organization, influencing the behavior of employees, volunteers, and board members. It makes a difference when the executive director enters a room with a smile and says good morning, welcoming junior and senior peers with equal interest. It helps to ask about families, to send congratulatory notes or condolence cards, to encourage departments to share lunch or celebrate birthdays together. These small acts of kindness create a climate where collegiality thrives and gossip, rumors, derogatory jokes, and sexist and racist behavior are all clearly unacceptable.

Beyond establishing the culture of the agency, I see five essential qualities for leadership within the not-for-profit world:

1. **Vision.** This is the ability to think big, to see the bigger picture. It enables a leader to move an organization above and beyond its perceived role and position. For example, when a homeless services organization starts to develop low-income housing, that represents vision.

2. **Commitment.** This involves believing in what the organization stands for even during difficult times. It means being passionate about the purpose and mission of the agency. Think of organizations promoting intergroup relations, not only today but also during the civil rights era.

3. **Excellence.** Leaders are always on a quest for mastery. They hold the bar high, showing all employees that excellence is something to strive for. They give praise and reward superior performance.

4. **Humility.** The executive should not see herself as better than others or as holding beliefs that are more important than those of her colleagues. Humility allows for openness, self-criticism, and reflection. One way to demonstrate humility is to hold regular forums or town meetings where staff can offer ideas, suggestions, and constructive criticism.

5. **Peace of Mind.** Here I quote Dr. Raymond T. Yeh of the University of Texas from *Association Executive* magazine: "Leaders have a deep sense of satisfaction about what they have done to make a difference in the world. They have gained the peace of mind that comes from knowing that when their best was called upon, they delivered.... They have a heightened awareness of their own being."

Beyond these qualities, the executive director has a number of tools to help her lead. Here are a few tips, some my own, others gleaned from Dr. Barton Goldsmith, a consultant and speaker on leadership who has also written for *Association Executive*:

1. **Send your message.** Communicate your thoughts and ideas clearly and frequently and motivate others to do the same.

2. **Understand behavior.** Feelings are just as important as conduct in the workplace.

3. **Express emotion.** If you're facing issues of significance, don't be afraid to convey passion or, where appropriate, indignation.

4. **Motivate staff.** The leader has no greater responsibility than the development of others.

5. **Create a learning environment.** See yourself as an educator in addition to being a manager.

6. **Think big, act small.** Do not micro-manage but understand that any organization lives or dies on accomplishing the "details of the work."

7. **Be a "yes" person, not a naysayer.** Find ways to say yes even if the yes needs to be limited or modified.

8. **Develop a team approach.** See yourself as the conductor of an orchestra where every musician must perform together to create perfect harmony.

9. **Create clear practices and standards.** Make sure you have a good human resources department or a set of personnel practices and standards. Involve staff in its creation and assessment of performance.

10. **Do not punish failure** when it was done with good intentions as part of an attempt to try new approaches. Learn from it.

Leading the Staff: Integrating Approaches to Leadership

Many people see two clear styles of leadership: authoritarian and autocratic or participatory and democratic. Max Weber, a famous social scientist from the early twentieth century, characterized these different styles as vertical and horizontal. Both are necessary. The not-for-profit executive needs to be a figure of authority without being authoritarian, a person of strength without being a strong man. The most central challenge is serving as a catalyst, inspiring the staff to reach their full potential.

Vertical leadership strengthens the role of the top executive in setting direction, standards, and policy, and is often referred to as "top down" management. The horizontal approach is more collegial, invests more authority to others, and involves considerable power-sharing. Neither approach, on its own, is ideal.

Agency executives who yield too much power and authority to others in the horizontal model often abdicate their responsibility to lead. They are fearful of the consequences and responsibilities that accompany decision-making and therefore delegate it to others. On the other hand, executives who only pronounce from above and expect people to follow do not understand the importance of engaging every person on every branch in the tree of responsibility.

The executive has to find the proper balance. She has to know when to delegate and when to make decisions herself. She needs to share authority and power, but she also needs to know when to intervene. Everyone knows the joke about the difficult, perplexing, or daunting issue that comes up, only to be referred to committee, where it will languish forever. Instead of dodging responsibility, a good executive director addresses those issues directly, leading vertically.

Other instances call for the horizontal approach. I recently told some of our staff, who were busily drafting their annual budget, that I could have gone into my office, locked the door, worked for three hours, and devised essentially the same document that was taking them weeks and months to prepare and finalize. Why not do it that way and save lots of time? Because in so doing, you deny your staff an opportunity to own the process, to be involved in the development of such an important instrument, to learn from their participation and feel empowered that they struggled, invested, and ultimately defined their own budget.

The best leaders bring out the best in their staff.

I've always tried to hire staff from the communities we serve and to offer opportunities for professional development. I think of Casper Lassiter, a young African-American who came to our Dunlevy Milbank community center in Harlem starting at age nine, when he was living with his grandmother in an apartment on the same block as the center. Casper's mother was struggling to make ends meet and his father was in prison, but between his grandmother, his uncles, his extended family at Milbank, and his own hard work, Casper thrived. He excelled in our basketball league, joined our teen pregnancy prevention program, and earned his first paycheck selling hot dogs as part of an entrepreneurial club at Milbank. Thanks in part to the connections he made in our basketball league, he earned a sports scholarship to the Salisbury School, a private high school in Connecticut. When it was time for college, Children's Aid provided modest scholarship support to help him attend Lehigh University, where he studied social psychology and theater, and we later provided a staff scholarship when he attended the Hunter College Graduate School of Social Work. We are lucky indeed that he has chosen to remain with us, working today as the assistant director at Milbank. He is married, the father of a six-month-old son and two girls, ages ten and seven, who now also attend our programs.

Leaders who are catalysts help employees at all levels figure out what they need to thrive. For messengers, that might mean providing an on-the-job mentor and offering a flexible schedule so they can finish a high school degree. For senior executives, it might mean employment arrangements that make it possible to simultaneously lecture or consult, or simply providing the autonomy they need to bring programs to new heights. Catalysts constantly encourage their staff to learn, share ideas, experiment, and expand their intellectual horizons.

Instead of thinking of leadership as strictly horizontal or vertical, executive directors should take a more nuanced approach that incorporates elements of both. Even more important, leaders should consistently strive to create an environment that sparks personal and institutional growth.

Encouraging High-Level Performance and Morale

It's not fashionable these days to admit that we are drawn to people who possess power and are bold and forthright in its use, but surely we are. Even the professional literature over the years has spoken of leadership as constituting three interconnected systems: power, affection, and communication. All three elements deserve closer attention.

Power, if used correctly, is necessary for the implementation of an agency's goals. The communication system, formal and informal, is equally important. This is as true in the age of the Internet as it was in the era of the mimeograph machine. Affection is also crucial: leaders need to be liked and to share positive feelings toward others. The leader who is strong but despised is isolated and ineffective. The leader who is liked but not strong is seen as spineless. Lastly, leaders who are likable and strong but do not know how to share, delegate, distribute, and reward are also ineffective.

Communication and affection are often intertwined, as is the case with staff development. Salaries are never the sole reason people remain on the job. High turnover is the bane of the not-for-profit manager, and we all know that even when compensation levels are adequate, they are not enough to retain staff over the long haul.

What else is needed? Over time, I've found that employees stay with an agency when they believe the agency cares about them, that it is committed not only to its mission but also to its employees. Staff members want to be a part of the executive director's work family. They want to be known and noticed, admired and respected. In smaller organizations, the executive should take the time to know every employee. In larger organizations, the executive should still try to know each employee's name and can create a caring environment through institutional arrangements. This can include an employee assistance program that provides counseling for staff coping with serious issues like divorce and the death of a loved one. It can also include a scholarship program to support professional development. Other helpful steps include flexible work arrangements for new parents and compassionate policies providing medical leave and time off to care for ailing relatives. At The Children's Aid Society, we also implemented a domestic violence prevention program with the help of my wife, Lynn Harman, an attorney who established such a program in her for-profit company. This proved useful not only for our clients but also for many of our staff.

An effective leader also opens the channels of communication with staff members, encouraging them to think independently. Staff should feel they can express their ideas within their department—and directly to management. A leader is a change agent, and a change agent looks critically not only at our larger society but also at her own agency, seeing it as a dynamic, ever-changing organism. Staff members can help create change by setting up committees to address issues and policies of concern. This should be more than an out-let for frustration. Have the foresight and the courage to follow through and change dysfunctional systems—we all have them, and only through an effort by all involved will we improve or replace them.

Each organization has different needs and different budgets, yet even in difficult times, the executive director cannot ignore the importance of providing tangible support for work that goes above and beyond the call of duty. Incentive pay and modest bonuses are crucial to the process. Another useful measure is establishing an employee excellence award program, which institutionalizes a commitment to excellence at all levels, from professionals to support staff to maintenance workers. This program, which we initiated at Children's

Aid fifteen years ago, involves a small monetary award and a citation; employees attend a ceremony, often accompanied by family members, where their supervisor lauds their accomplishments. To recognize the importance of their efforts, I always attend along with our board president or chairman.

I also believe very strongly in interacting directly with staff. Visiting the various work sites, floor by floor or building by building, has always been part of my regular routine, especially on evenings, weekends, and holidays, when staff give up their personal time to provide around-the-clock support for clients. It is amazing to see how much staff members appreciate it when the executive director visits on Thanksgiving or Christmas morning, at nine in the evening, or on a Sunday afternoon. A visit of this sort shows front-line staff that they are not alone in their work, that the executive travels along the same path that they do. It shows how deeply the director values their contributions.

An old camp director of mine would say, "Smile.

It only takes six muscles. Frowning takes over 300." I agree. It's so easy to give recognition and to spend a few hours in the field. It cheers you up, it inspires the staff, and it's always more productive than locking yourself in the office with budget sheets.

Risks and Rewards

Right around 1970, before the advent of *Roe v. Wade* in 1973, there was a short, sharp spike in the incidence of teen births in the United States. At The Children's Aid Society, we didn't need to review the data—we saw the situation firsthand throughout our programs and services, where our staff were increasingly at the receiving end of sensitive questions about contraception, sexually transmitted diseases, and illegal abortions. This led, in turn, to questions directed to the top: What was our position? Where did we stand? How best could we help teens who trusted us to provide sound advice?

Instead of ignoring or avoiding teen sexuality—a politically charged topic, then and now—we chose to take a risk and address the issue directly. It was indeed fortuitous that I had been introduced by a mutual friend to Michael Carrera, who earned his doctorate in health sciences with a specialty in human sexuality. I passed on the questions from our staff to Mike, and his answers were so useful and insightful that I knew he had to join us. He was a professor at Hunter College, on his way to becoming a national expert on sexuality education, but I was able to hire him part-time, and he eventually developed an "above the waist" teen pregnancy prevention program that is intensive, comprehensive, and not inexpensive. It is also highly controversial.

Let me step back for a moment to describe the program, which is now adapted or replicated in about fifty locations nationwide and does much more than prevent pregnancies. Children join at age eleven and continue until high school, attending workshops six days a week for fifty weeks a year. Mike now runs the program full-time, and he advocates a "lifeguard" approach, jumping in and doing everything humanly possible to help participants succeed. As he puts it, "Hope is a powerful contraceptive. The way that you help young people avoid pregnancy is by providing them with real evidence that good things can happen in their lives."

We provide this evidence through academic assistance, job training, mental health services, sports and arts classes, and medical and dental care. None of this raises alarm. Yet the program also includes unusually clear and direct discussions of family and adolescent sexuality. Our counselors advise young people to wait to become sexually active, but they do not reject teens who ignore the advice, and instead offer practical information on how to avoid pregnancies; when they do occur, counselors provide information on the full range of options. Pregnancies have been a rare outcome over the two decades of the program. This program was risky for the agency when we started and it remains risky today, especially in a time when "abstinence only" is the government's preferred approach.

Yet this risk has led to incredible rewards, especially for the thousands of young people who have graduated from the program. A three-year evaluation, conducted by Philliber Research Associates, found that ours is the only program in the country working with teens in disadvantaged communities that has achieved reductions in both pregnancies and births. In fact, teen girls in our group were nearly fifty percent less likely to experience pregnancy and births than teen girls in the control group.

This extraordinary success underscores the importance of standing up for principles and taking risks in programming, even if it means forgoing government funding for this program for more than twenty years.

Another level of risk involves honestly confronting dysfunction and failure within programs and services, and sharing issues directly with staff and board members. At the board level, it's much easier to put on a monthly "dog and pony" show that highlights stellar programs and services—but even the best organizations have weak spots, and the board needs to know where they are.

The board should also understand the risks and exposures that accompany governance—and this isn't just about proper bylaws, current directors' and officers' insurance, and compliance with Sarbanes-Oxley. The real risks involve the work we do and the challenges that come with the work, from a child getting lost on a field trip, sexually molested by a guardian, or even dying while under the agency's care. Despite all our efforts, crises can and do occur, and they shouldn't take board members by surprise.

Painting a true picture can be painful, but it does offer benefits. It creates a sense of teamwork and gives the board and staff the opportunity to join the executive in solving crises and problems. It also builds trust—if the staff and the board see that you accurately assess risk, it helps them feel better prepared. It can't be stressed too often: open communication is essential for a strong and effective organization.

Valuing and Working with Volunteers

The executive director's job includes making sure that the entire work family, including volunteers, feels wanted and has a place at the table. Many organizations make the mistake of treating volunteers like an unwanted relative, but in my view they deserve an honored place among professionals.

Volunteers are a large and diverse group of individuals, and it's wise to pay attention to all of them. I include our trustees and donors in this group. They all give without expecting to receive; their only compensation is the reward that comes from helping others. I also include the more typical volunteers: the tutors, the mentors, the Little League coaches, the event planners and party organizers, the folks who take children on trips and collect toys for holiday distribution. This group also includes the partners, spouses, and children of the professionals, who in some instances give almost as many hours to the organization as their employed relatives.

I want to underscore the importance of community volunteers. They can be parents who supervise the
snack time in an after-school program, grandparents
raising their grandchildren who provide support to
others in the same situation, and teens leading a community service group. They can also be local leaders:
the police officer who runs a softball league, the minister who oversees a canned food drive for the homeless. Community volunteers add power and authen-
ticity to our voice. Their faces become a part of our
image and reputation in the community, with multiple positive effects.

Honoring volunteers calls for more than an annual appreciation dinner. The executive director and
the staff need to respect their efforts and good intentions by providing for them a sense of the professional-
ism that the organization represents. What exactly does
this involve? Well, little things like coming on time to
meetings, having the room ready and available, being
friendly and gracious, and offering tea and cookies if

it is an off-hour meeting. If the volunteer is a mentor, staff members should ensure that the mentee knows the time and the place of the encounter. If it is a Saturday bowling trip with children, staff should make sure to provide the permits and the petty cash to cover transportation or other incidentals.

These little things don't happen by accident. They require training for volunteers and staff, preferably by a dedicated staff member. While it may initially seem time-consuming and costly, I have found that investing in volunteer services, ideally by hiring a dedicated volunteer services staff person, is worth every penny. It ensures that volunteers will get the training and ongoing oversight they need, and the same is true for professional staff, who need to understand how to provide structure, supervision, and clearly defined roles for volunteers without feeling overworked or overburdened. In some cases, part-time staff may even feel threatened that volunteers might take their job. A volunteer services professional will help ease these fears.

Volunteers get involved for a variety of reasons. Some want to give back, others want to socialize or make business connections. Still others want to help their own children, family, and community. In all instances, it's our job to give them a positive feeling about their interactions with our clients and our staff. If we do, our effort will be returned many times over in contributions of time and money, not just from volunteers but also from their friends and families. If we do not, volunteers will leave the agency and look elsewhere for other opportunities.

Diversity: Moving From Rhetoric to Reality

Believing in diversity is like breathing for me: it's a part of who I am, a reflection of my upbringing and my involvement in social justice struggles over a number of decades. These days, almost everyone supports equality of opportunity and opposes discrimination, but bringing these lofty ideals to ground-level reality still remains extremely challenging.

I've been lucky to lead an organization with a long history of serving not only the offspring of Irish, Italian, and German immigrants but also the children of African-Americans and more recent newcomers from the Caribbean, Central and South America, Asia, and the Middle East. Our famous "alumni" include not only Al Pacino but also Bayard Rustin, Harry Belafonte, Langston Hughes, and Thelonious Monk. Even so, the front-line staff, senior management, and board of directors of the organization I joined in 1966 did not fully represent the communities we served or our commitment to pluralism.

One of my goals at Children's Aid has been to improve our diversity. This took many forms, from integrating a summer sleepaway camp to hiring more African-American and Latino managers to bringing more women and people from the communities we serve to our board. It also involved a zero tolerance policy toward any form of discrimination or bias, internal or external, with repercussions including censure and dismissal when charges were found to be true.

Every not-for-profit director should assess the gap between the rhetoric and reality of diversity within her organization. She should go above and beyond the measures required by law and include unequivocal anti-discrimination statements in the organization's code of conduct, personnel practices manual, and by-laws. She should ensure that hiring practices and promotional opportunities are blind to race, religion, ethnicity, gender, and sexual preference. Human resources personnel can support this process, but the executive director should be leading the call.

The Ethical Not-for-Profit Manager: Integrity Starts at the Top

The ethical manager understands that ethical behavior involves much more than statements, slogans, or codes. Instead, she behaves consciously and ethically herself and through her leadership creates a culture of integrity throughout the not-for-profit organization.

Ethical behavior and decision-making should per-meate daily working life. It's about confidentiality—keeping private documents within locked files and resisting the urge to gossip or start rumors. It's about honesty—clearly stating goals, working diligently to meet them and admitting failures when they occur. It's also about decency—treating clients and colleagues with respect, never stooping to make random com-ments about looks, weight, or physical presence.

Of course, there are a few gray areas. Should a major donor expect that his or her son or daughter will receive a paid internship or entry-level employ-ment? What about an employee who is found to be negligent in his child support payments? How do we respond when a social worker becomes so involved with a foster child that she starts to talk about adopt-ing him? Each of these cases needs to be dealt with openly and on an individual basis. If we are thoughtful about small concerns, we will also keep our eyes and ears open for more substantial malfeasance.

An agency-wide code of conduct can and should reinforce sound ethics, but on its own it is not sufficient. The importance of ethical behavior needs to be constantly reinforced, cannot be taken for granted, cannot be dealt with once a year at an all-staff meeting.

In the corporate world, much attention is paid to employees' appearance. While I understand the importance of professional attire, I am much more concerned with whether my staff is sincere, honest, and respectful of the people with whom we work. When visitors arrive, they should immediately sense a warm and welcoming atmosphere. From the supervisor to the social worker to the messenger, we all need to exemplify the most esteemed values of our not-for-profit organization.

The significance of ethical behavior cannot be overstated. The lifeblood of the not-for-profit is trust. If that trust is broken, years of goodwill and good work are destroyed.

Taking Care of Yourself

The executive director's job, if done well, is stressful. The active executive lives the job, and it's always with her. She runs the agency, supports the staff, interacts with the board, raises the dollars, works with government, solves the problems, and confronts the crises. She is often bombarded with questions, issues, and problems, yet she needs to remain approachable, accessible, and—most of the time—calm. To avoid burnout, the executive needs to pay attention to her physical and emotional well-being.

Not everyone follows this advice, including yours truly. As Mark Twain famously put it, "To do the right thing is noble—to advise others to do the right thing is also noble and a lot easier." For most of my forty years at The Children's Aid Society, I would have to describe myself as a workaholic. I woke up at 3 a.m. worrying about personnel issues, I worked all day, I attended evening events, and I returned home late at night. I spent every Saturday until 3 p.m. visiting our various facilities in Manhattan, Brooklyn, the Bronx, and Staten Island. My "Monday memos" reporting on my activities—the Early Head Start graduation that brought me near to tears, the grubby bathroom in one of our centers that I mopped and cleaned myself—were infamous among my senior staff. I was able to keep up this relentless pace not only because of my own drive and sense of responsibility but also through the support of my children and my late wife, Kay Coltoff, who often accompanied me on my Saturday "rounds." After Kay's death, I remarried, and my second wife, Lynn Harman, accepting and understanding my role, was also most supportive. Frankly, I don't think I could have done this work without the encouragement of both Kay and Lynn. By the time I married Lynn, I realized that four nights a week and Saturday was a bit too much, and I reduced my workload. I knew in my gut that senior staff would pick up where I left off—and do as good a job, if not better.

During the years when I was working long hours, I

understood I needed to relax. Sometimes I forced myself to stay home on Saturdays, but I found myself feeling guilty if I wasn't in the field. I tried to meditate on
the commuter train going home, but all too often I fell
asleep. I attempted yoga years before it became a craze,
but my conscious was battling my subconscious, and
instead of focusing on my breathing I kept returning to
concerns about work. I've always been single-minded
in my devotion to work and believe in setting the bar
high to inspire others. Nonetheless, as we all know, a
never-ending work schedule takes a serious toll on relationships with family and friends. We have to fulfill
our responsibilities, but we also need to set limits.

This is helpful on another level. For the executive
director to remain the go-to person, she must ensure
that she is not so overburdened or anxious that the
staff feel sorry for her and choose not to make any further demands on her time. That is exactly what we do
not want to occur. The key is spending time on team-
building and learning how and when to delegate.

Every executive director should take the time to understand how she best copes with stress, whether it's a stroll around the block, slamming a squash ball, or enjoying classical music. Every executive director should seek counsel and support from those she trusts. She should make sure that she eats well, sleeps well, and takes time out for recreation and for periods of relaxing and recharging. Vacations are not a matter of choice but of necessity. Now that I take them, I know. Everyone benefits when the top executive achieves a sense of balance and equilibrium.

Key Points

- Executive directors profoundly influence the culture of their organization. They should be a model of respect, collegiality, and a commitment to excellence.

- The best executive directors integrate elements of both "vertical" and "horizontal" leadership, striking a healthy balance between delegating responsibility and taking charge.

- An effective leader creates an environment that encourages employees to succeed and commit for the long haul.

- Spending time on the front lines with staff members is a powerful morale booster. It shows employees how much the director values their time and commitment.

- Leaders are willing to take thoughtful risks and stand up for principles, even if such positions are controversial.

- Volunteers are vitally important in the life of not-for-profits. They should not be taken for granted and should receive training, support, and recognition.

- Executive directors need to continuously promote diversity, addressing the gap between rhetoric and reality within their organizations.

- In the not-for-profit environment, ethics are an every day concern. The executive director needs to exemplify the highest standards of ethical behavior and enforce a code of conduct.

- Leadership takes a toll. Finding the balance between home and work is essential.

CHAPTER 4

External Relations

The Not-for-Profit as Social Safety Net

As not-for-profits have grown larger and more professional, we have stepped forward to meet the greater needs and growing numbers of the disenfranchised. We serve the young and the old, the able-bodied and the disabled, the poor and the middle-class, the new arrivals and the established residents, working together with every racial, ethnic, and religious group imaginable. Working in partnership with the government, we are indeed the social safety net of the nation.

The not-for-profit sector is crucial to our society. Could cities function without the existence of not-for-profit medical centers, universities, nursing homes, assisted-living facilities, children's camps, institutions for the disabled, Boys & Girls Clubs, Ys, and Little

Leagues? Could small towns thrive without a volunteer fire department, ambulance service, or Girl Scouts? Our society is truly built on voluntary efforts. In fact, the United States has the world's most elaborate systems of nongovernmental higher education and health and social services.

Yet the government has always shaped our development. As American society industrialized, the church-based "charity movement," as large as it was, could not keep up with the needs of our citizens. The hardship of the Great Depression created popular support for government assistance, laying the groundwork for what eventually became the Social Security Administration, workers' compensation, unemployment insurance, disability coverage, Medicare, and Medicaid. Along the way, the government also started funding education, health-care, day-care, and other services, and in some instances it provided those services directly. Over time, however, all levels of government—federal, state, and city—have reduced direct services and contracted out much of the work to not-for-profits. It has become generally accepted that a smaller, better-managed, less bureaucratic not-for-profit does the job with greater care and at lesser cost.

Today, many not-for-profits could not survive without government financing. This symbiotic relationship is like a marriage. Sometimes it falters at the altar. Other times, it is consummated but annulled rather quickly. In a best-case scenario, it is a bond that benefits both sides and withstands the test of time.

But even the best partnerships show signs of stress during budget season. Government officials can be fickle partners: they giveth and they taketh away. When times are good, they are more generous, and when times are bad they are parsimonious. Unfortunately, most of the time, times are bad. It is rare at any level of government to hear officials say, "We have more money than we know what to do with." When times are truly bad, services to the poor generally get reduced or eliminated first. Our clients represent the least powerful constituency in terms of voting and political action. Despite our best efforts, in recent decades there have been significant cutbacks in foster care and adoption services, day-care funding, after-school programming, and, of late, key health and mental health services.

The strain between government and not-for-profit organizations will always exist because our interests are not always compatible. Even the most thoughtful and compassionate official must meet the demands for cutbacks or retrenchments. The government bureaucrat is usually more interested in maintaining control and authority, unwilling to rock the boat and risk job security to fight for the needs of the poor. That's the reality of "Where you stand depends on where you sit."

This reality also affects some of my positions. Even though I support family preservation policies, which keep children with their biological parents even when there are troubling signs about the family's stability, I have spent decades advocating that if those troubling signs continue, children should be removed from their homes and placed in a safe environment until a more complete investigation is conducted. If I worked in government, there would be considerably more pressure for me to follow the current party line.

In the final analysis, the not-for-profit is a dependent partner in the marriage with government agencies. We should continue influencing government to make it a more consistent, sustaining partner. Yet at the same time, it's helpful, even essential, to diversify funding sources.

Fundraising and Funders: Tips from the Field

When I entered the field of social work, the last thing on my mind was raising money. However, when I look back at my years as executive director, fundraising has been one of my most important and satisfying responsibilities. The new not-for-profit executive needs to embrace this part of the job if he wants to create a legacy of change, innovation, and growth.

This is a break from the past, when many boards had complete control and responsibility for fundraising. Today, however, the executive director in most not-for-profits oversees the budget process and all fiscal matters, including fundraising.

In some organizations, the chief financial officer and the development director appear to have almost as much authority as the executive director. This is a mistake that dilutes the executive director's ability to manage the agency. These positions, while powerful, should be subordinate to the chief executive. This division of power is essential: employees need to know that the chain of command goes up to the executive director—and none other.

Historically, fundraising was a board function. Board members had the contacts and knew the right people in society and foundations. While the board still plays an important role in fundraising and should continue to do so, the executive director is often one of the key fundraisers. As executives become more prominent, they develop their own contacts in the community of funders, not only government agencies but also individual donors, corporate foundations, family foundations, and philanthropic foundations. The executive gets to know the people who are running these foundations, is connected to the umbrella organizations like the United Way and the Community Chest and becomes a principal fundraiser. I think that's good. While it means more work, it provides leverage for the director with the board and with funders because he is not only the one who spends the dollars but also the one who raises them.

Most people are uncomfortable asking for money. Here are some of the lessons I learned from Truda C. Jewett, who served for more than a decade as our assistant executive director for development and is known as the best professional pickpocket in town.

1. **Get Out of the Office.** Be active and make a point of meeting one-on-one, face-to-face, with major

donors and foundation directors. Funders may say they want to know and understand your organization, but in the final analysis they give to a person—you. They need to know who you are.

2. **Keep in Constant Contact.** Follow up on your meetings with a steady stream of written material—not just annual reports and newsletters but also white papers, evaluation reports, and press clippings. Show them you're at the front of the pack. If new funding comes along, you want them to think of you first. If they're shifting their priorities, you want them to ask you for advice.

3. **Deal with Funders as Equals.** Most major foundations are run by professionals. You are their peer, and they want to deal with you. Project the same attitude with wealthy donors, regardless of their net worth. If the work you are doing is exciting and important, they will want to get involved.

4. **Treat Individual Donors as Individuals.** Follow up with big donors the same way you would with major

foundations, but add a personal touch. Take the time to get to know them—invite them to lunch, to site visits, to board meetings, to agency events, to presentations by senior staff. Bring them into your "work family" and let them know the importance of their support. Be sensitive to their personal style—some donors want a lot of recognition while others prefer to remain behind the scenes.

The popular image of fundraising involves only private sources. Yet government revenue in the form of contracts and other arrangements often represents the lion's share of an agency's income. Thus, bringing in government contracts is also a form of fundraising, one that usually falls to the executive director. The board and the senior staff should know when the executive director is a major player in securing revenue, whether it's public or private. Additional recognition and respect follows when the board and staff know that he is also a significant player in raising funds.

In recent years, deferred giving arrangements in the form of charitable remainder trusts, unitrusts, mini-trusts, and bequests have become ever more important for long-term financing. The executive should be involved in this process even if the agency outsources some of the detail work. In large agencies, deferred giving is part of the development office, but the executive director needs to be involved in creating the message and meeting with representatives of trusts and banks and with individuals who are considering leaving bequests.

Many not-for-profits have also begun to pay attention to creating and sustaining an endowment, which is just another name for a reserve fund or a rainy-day fund. While universities, religious institutions, and large cultural and medical centers have always known the importance of endowments, social service and youth-serving agencies have only recently begun to recognize this. For years, our leaders thought that every penny should be spent on services. When it's a struggle just to make payroll, it's hard to think beyond the here and now. Nonetheless, government contracts are never secure, and only if the agency has reserve funds can shortfalls be filled without slashing programs and penalizing clients. Executive directors should work closely with their boards, helping them to understand the importance of an endowment and initiating capital campaigns either to develop or add to their reserve funds. To be comfortable, it is suggested that these funds in reserve should be two to three times the size of the annual budget.

Fundraising Facts of Life

Relationships with funders can be tricky. The best ones evolve over time, through years of one-on-one meetings, leading not only to mutual respect and understanding but also to a steady stream of reliable funding. I was recently thrilled to work with a longtime funder who was so impressed by our work that he provided a considerable grant for an internship/externship program that helped our staff members document their "best practices" and pass them on to other organizations. We developed the program in partnership with the funder, but he left all the details to us.

Alas, it doesn't always work this way. In a growing number of instances, major private foundations are requesting an unusually large measure of control over the programs they support, from creation to content to supervision. Some funders cherish the partnership with the provider and work productively, side-by-side, to enhance the program. Others are so picky and intrusive that they truly drive the not-for-profit to distraction. Enough already! Funders need to respect the independence of the not-for-profit. They should not determine mission, program content, priorities, or staff development and training. These areas are the agency's responsibility under the direction of the executive director.

When working with funders, always remember that they have their own agenda and their own board to satisfy. If their agenda aligns with yours, it may be fine to allow involvement and some measure of control. However, if an executive director begins to accept dollars that call for work beyond the boundaries of the agency's mission, problems can and will develop. Do not get stuck in an overly narrow definition of mission, but do apply careful consideration and sound judgment when funding comes with too many strings attached. Sometimes all that is necessary is a meeting in person with a funder to clarify your position. On rare occasions, it's best to turn down a gift.

To give funders credit, one of the most positive developments in our field has been their support for collaborative projects. In large-scale community-building efforts, for example, a foundation may support housing, social service, and advocacy groups, encouraging them to work together to improve not only bricks and mortar but also the daily lives of children and families. Collaborative efforts are proliferating in schools, community centers, settlement houses, and health and mental health clinics, and they're almost always beneficial, integrating services and avoiding duplication. Nonetheless, we need to be aware of the immense work that goes on behind the scenes in collaborative efforts. They call for a heavy-duty commitment to the process of change—developing consensus, determining leadership, merging budgets, and sharing credit. The time and effort involved is considerable.

Another trend among foundations is giving support only for specific purposes like anti-obesity programs and intergenerational activities. These purposes change annually, and foundations want all the bells and whistles, identifiable outcomes, innovation, and replication. This is fine—to a point. The executive director should always be on the lookout for funders who will provide unrestricted dollars to cover management and overhead expenses. A key part of the job is educating funders, showing them that high-quality social services are dependent on the overall fiscal and administrative management of the agency. If I could gather every foundation official in the country into one room, here is the message I would blast out by megaphone: the most useful support is general operating support.

Working with Different Publics

The executive director's job has become ever more complex, and he must be ever-mindful of the different constituencies he serves: clients, staff, the board, the media, the government, the public at large. Throughout all of this work, the agency's image and the image of the chief executive should be one and the same.

This is not about ego gratification or self-promotion. Instead, it's about giving your agency a strong, clear, consistent image—or "brand," to use the corporate language. Executives who avoid publicity do their agency and themselves a disservice. Executives who are uncomfortable speaking in public or appearing on television are denying their agency a prime opportunity to explain their mission and comment on vital issues of the day. The executive director is a spokesperson. The more his face and voice are on television, in the press, and on the radio, the more the media think of him as an expert on social issues of local and national importance, and the better it is for the agency.

While sending our message, we need to be consistent yet aware of our different constituencies. What do I mean? The consistency part is fairly straightforward: it involves speaking clearly, to the point, and sending the same message regardless of your audience. Let me illustrate using my own position on the family preservation approach to child welfare, one that leaves the child with his or her family even if there are signs of neglect. While I understand the benefits of family preservation, I have also consistently spoken out about its limits. When danger signs emerge, children need to be removed and placed in foster care, despite its imperfections. For many years I have advocated this position at every opportunity, in the press and with public officials, regardless of how strongly an administration has been pushing for family preservation.

The differentiation part is about being sensitive to the way public comments come across, especially to public officials. Few people like surprises, and this is especially true for politicians and bureaucrats. When I plan to take a position on a highly charged and controversial issue, I try to find ways to inform my board and colleagues in government. Since The Children's Aid Society receives significant funding not only for foster care but also for support services for family preservation, taking a stand is undoubtedly a risk. Yet I have found that when government officials understand that my public posture is not a personal attack on them or their integrity but instead a legitimate and constructive position in public debate, they usually respect this and refrain from retaliation.

Some might argue that my ability to advocate for our clients is hobbled by my need to ensure continued government funding. I understand that position, but I disagree. Not fearing open communication, the executive builds relationships that enable him to share his ideas and public comments with professional colleagues, board members and staff in a respectful manner. There is no contradiction between being diplomatic and addressing principle.

Not-for-profit executives who stay on message, remain true to their principles, and do not yield or compromise to satisfy others are generally held in the highest esteem. Those who equivocate or use inflammatory language are dismissed as dilettantes and political opportunists.

Key Points

- Many not-for-profits depend on government financing, especially during the budget process. Fundraising from other sources helps to develop independence.

- Agencies need to develop a reserve fund or endowment.

- The executive director should be one of the principal fundraisers—both in the private and public sector.

- Some funders make excessive demands on not-for-profit organizations. To manage this often-tricky relationship, the executive director should establish clear boundaries between the funder and the agency.

- The executive director should be the public face and voice of the organization, speaking frequently and forcefully in public and effectively using the media.

- The executive director needs to deliver a consistent message while remaining sensitive to different constituencies.

CHAPTER 5
The Big Picture

Service Plus Advocacy Equals Change

A few years ago, I developed a brief phrase together with senior staff and board members that sums up the scope and mission of The Children's Aid Society: "Service Plus Advocacy Equals Change." This concept, which others sometimes describe as "case to cause," is useful far beyond our own organization. I'd like to detail each element of the equation:

Service. The primary function of most not-for-profits is delivering a service, in areas that extend from health and education to social, cultural, and family services, and far beyond. In most cases, service delivery is the reason the agency exists. At The Children's Aid Society, we reach about 150,000 children and families in the New York City area and countless more through various technical assistance and replication programs throughout the country.

Advocacy. Through advocacy, we expand our reach exponentially, taking what we have learned from our program results and research and expanding to scale. It may seem like Children's Aid serves a large number of people, but our reach pales in comparison to the 29 million children growing up poor in America. Advocacy requires a whole different set of skills from service delivery: report writing, press conferences, coalition-building, information sessions with legislators, marches, and demonstrations. Some of our best advocacy has involved the community schools program, which I described earlier. We've advocated our position on multiple fronts: through a multi-year Advertising Council campaign, through our participation in the creation of a national Coalition for Community Schools, through speeches and testimonials to legislatures around the country by the staff of our National Technical Assistance Center for Community Schools. Through vigorous advocacy, we have played a pivotal role in the development of a grassroots movement to add support services to schools all over the country. Working in partnership with others, especially the Coalition for Community Schools, we have influenced federal legislation, particularly the U.S. Department of Education's 21st Century Community Learning Centers program, which funds a wide array of after-school programs. Congress appropriated nearly $1 billion for the program in the 2005 fiscal year.

Change. The ultimate goal of advocacy is tangible change in policies and practices. We achieved this goal within our health care access program, which we initiated in 1998 to help uninsured children and families receive Medicaid or Child Health Plus through a process known as facilitated enrollment. Working on our own, we initially enrolled thousands of children and adults, without government support. We then expanded our efforts with state support, overseeing a coalition of community-based organizations committed to helping as many eligible families enroll as possible. By mid-2006 we had overseen the collective enrollment of 40,000 children and adults in New York City. In addition, the depth and breadth of our experience meant that local and state officials sought our input in policy formation. One of our main findings in this work was the excessive complexity of the enrollment process; we were pleased to help simplify state guidelines for the Child Health Insurance program, and our perspective was also included in the design of the state's Family Health Plus program. Our early commitment to this work, our extensive on-the-ground experience, and our collaborations with the Children's Defense Fund and many others have made us leaders in this field. We are pleased to have helped the State of New York reduce the number of unenrolled children and adults from about 800,000 to about 400,000 in less than a decade.

I hope you see my point. Service is the heart and soul of what we do. Advocacy involves presenting our best practices to the public, policy-makers, and politicians. Change occurs when our programs and perspectives reach a much larger audience. When all three elements are in place, it's a powerful equation.

Our work is most effective when we combine a solid understanding of service delivery with sophisticated knowledge of city, state, and federal policy-making. I have found that organizations that exist solely to advocate public policies have less influence with legislators than those that combine service delivery with advocacy. Legislators trust us because they know we have our "feet to the fire," not under a computer or a blackboard.

Capacity, Growth, and Management

It's easier to grow than to manage the growth. This truism cannot be repeated too often, especially in the not-for-profit arena. Growth looks good and sounds good—more employees, new sites, bigger budgets— but it isn't meaningful unless it is well managed. Before embarking on grand plans, the not-for-profit executive director needs to proceed with caution.

In our field, the possibilities for growth are as vast as the unmet needs of the people we serve. A group that serves disabled adults expands to serve disabled children. A neighborhood-based AIDS organization opens new offices throughout the city. An agency that provides employment advice to new immigrants adds referrals for health-care and child-care to its services.

In theory, organizational growth and development should be slow and steady, proactively following the outlines developed in a strategic plan. Of course, the reality is often the opposite—far too many not-for-profits expand quickly and haphazardly in response to new government contracts or priorities developed by private funders.

When opportunities arise, executives need to ask: Does this growth fit within our mission? Where will it make an impact? Will we still provide high-quality services? Can we sustain the growth over time?

In my last decade leading The Children's Aid Society, we experienced an extended period of growth, adding new community schools, new health services, new programs for juvenile offenders, and a large new multi-service center in the South Bronx. To ensure high-quality services, we didn't just open site offices and hire front-line staff. We also made a substantial investment in new senior managers, some with national experience. Further steps included improving our infrastructure, completing an agency-wide technology upgrade, creating a centralized human resources department, and installing state-of-the-art accounting software.

We appeared to be taking all the right steps to manage our growth—but we didn't do quite enough thinking about sustainability, neglecting to consider the long-term pension implications of adding several hundred new employees. Since we are on a defined benefit plan, the costs escalated. This was an unpleasant surprise, but one we can live with. Looking back, we should have factored these long-term costs into our plans and built them into our requests for grants and contracts.

A new expansion opportunity recently arose in the South Bronx and we decided to pass. After so many years marching forward, we needed to catch our breath and consolidate our services. Social service professionals always want to do more. But this heartfelt desire should not eclipse sound management and fiscal responsibility.

Damage Control: Expecting the Unexpected

Over the course of my career, a number of crises stand out clearly: coping with the World Trade Center attack and its devastating effect on the children and families we serve, confronting the crack epidemic right inside our community centers, responding to the plight of hundreds of homeless families living in chaos in the Prince George welfare hotel in Midtown Manhattan.

In each of these instances—and many others—I lived with the crisis day and night, often consumed by anxiety about how best to respond. But no matter how tense I was internally, I always tried to project an outward sense of resolve. My confidence comforted colleagues and clients, helping us truly focus and move forward.

Dealing with crises is a crucial part of the not-for-profit director's job description. As hard as we try, as clearly as we define and delegate responsibility, as much as we put safety measures in place, crises will develop, as sure as death and taxes. To manage a crisis, the chief executive must look at the whole situation, assess it, and then attempt to fix it. Sometimes this involves bringing together the staff and the board, but the ultimate responsibility lies with the director. Many situations require adjusting priorities and budgets without delay.

Crises are always a test of leadership. Amid the shock and despair after the attack on the World Trade Center, it quickly became clear that even though The

Children's Aid Society isn't a traditional emergency relief agency, the children and families we serve had an immediate and urgent need for our help. In the first days and weeks after the attack, we kept our schools and community centers open to give people a place to come together and share their fears and feelings. We deployed our doctors, nurses, psychiatrists, and social workers to support grieving victims, and we created partnerships with unions to help the families of janitors, window washers, and waiters who lost their lives or their jobs. We quickly set up a World Trade Center relief office and over time collected, distributed, and committed more than $25 million, with more than $7 million coming from the New York Times 9/11 Neediest Fund under the leadership of Jack Rosenthal, president of the New York Times Company Foundation. I'm extraordinarily proud of the above-and-beyond effort put in by each and every member of our staff.

Yet some crises make you question your leadership. I'm thinking of the loss of a key government contract, nasty disputes on the board, or bad hiring decisions, especially at the senior level. It's natural to feel guilt and anger and to cast about for blame, but it's better to respond with a clear head and calm demeanor. When the crisis has passed, conduct a postmortem and learn from what went wrong.

Some of the most serious crises—the ones I woke up worrying about for decades—involve children in our care. Tragedy is always a possibility: on the jungle gym, in the pool, on the bus to summer camp. It is an even greater concern when you work with children in foster care, especially babies and young children with chronic medical conditions. Under my watch at Children's Aid, we didn't lose any children due to neglect, abuse, or poor judgments about foster care placements. Yet a number of very fragile children in our specialized medical foster care program died because of seizures and other natural causes. As director, I chose to console the foster families and birth families, arrange funerals and help our staff cope with profound grief and loss.

While these deaths were unpredictable and unavoidable, when asked about the hardest moments of the past forty years, I always remember the children we lost.

Key Points

- To make a lasting impact on policy and practice, consider this equation: service plus advocacy equals change.

- Bigger isn't always better. Growing a not-for-profit organization requires sound planning and oversight.

- Crises are always a test of leadership. They call for a calm, clear mind, and a willingness to adapt quickly and creatively to new and unexpected circumstances.

- After a crisis has passed, it is important to conduct a postmortem to learn from what went wrong.

CHAPTER 6
The Final Challenge

Retiring, Not Expiring

All executives move on. It's a painful fact of life, even in the best situations. This I know from experience, having recently stepped down as CEO and shifted to a consulting, advising, and fundraising position at Children's Aid. I hope that by recounting my experience it will ease the process for others.

Many executives resist planning for succession, clinging to the false hope that they will remain in top form, physically and mentally, well into their seventies. Many executives, especially men, seem to prefer expiring at the office to making the challenging transition to retirement. While understandable, this resistance is harmful, creating a climate of confusion and uncertainty that slows organizational growth and progress.

After I reached an appropriate age, the board and I

realized it was time to discuss succession. This process took place over many months, and I was closely involved throughout. Instead of undertaking an outside search, we chose to promote our able and experienced chief operating officer, C. Warren ("Pete") Moses. We announced the news at our annual board meeting and also informed staff, professional colleagues, funders, and the public. The announcement stated that Pete would immediately have an interim title—executive director—and that after a period of several years, I would step down and he would assume the position of chief executive officer.

The transition process was essential, giving the board, staff, and colleagues a chance to see Pete in a new role with new authority and responsibilities. I introduced Pete to important funders and government officials and briefed him on confidential aspects of the organization. It seemed like we handled the transition appropriately—clearly, carefully, purposefully.

So why did I find the process so difficult? Despite

my background in social work and my experience as a clinician, I became so focused on the operational aspects of the transition that I failed to deeply consider its emotional effects. What would it feel like to give up responsibility and authority after so many years as the ultimate decision-maker? How would Pete feel moving from second in command into a new light that is much brighter and more visible? What exactly was my new role and function within the organization? How would staff loyalties and allegiances change in response to the new pecking order? How would I feel watching the board members shift their attention to the new executive?

While I did spend some time considering these questions, I'm not sure I adequately prepared myself. The intellectual and the emotional are not seamless. The loss of a sense of belonging, of authority, of status, of control, even of friendship was enormous and engulfing. I felt I was giving up my "family" and experienced all the emotions that accompany such a fracture.

Frankly, it felt like grief. Luckily, the intensity of my emotions subsided after I took the time to explore and understand them.

I also thought a lot about what Pete must be experiencing. Although I had envisioned a close working relationship after I stepped down, we had fewer interactions than I had originally expected. Despite my expertise and long institutional memory, I realized that after many years as second in command, Pete was more than ready to take charge and do things his way. All those years of being my subordinate, of being subjected to my occasional criticism, of being asked to do tasks he did not wish to do, curbed some of his innate leadership. So when he assumed power, he came fully into himself.

The stress and strain of this time was not expressed in words. Instead, practical decisions, like the location of my office, assumed great symbolic value. Now that my office has been moved to a new location, I appreciate my light and airy new work space. I also appreciate that Pete needs his "space" to lead on his own terms.

In business and the professional world, CEOs who step down often continue on a consulting or limited-partner basis. In academia, emeritus is a common title offered to those distinguished faculty. In the not-for-profit world, the retiring CEO has much to offer the organization, and I would recommend, despite transitional difficulties, that more organizations consider such arrangements.

I mention all this to try and present a true picture of transitions. We need to understand what takes place in the merry-go-round of change, to anticipate some of the difficulties that inevitably accompany shifts in power, control, and status.

My father-in-law, Dr. Sidney Harman, who founded and still runs Harman International Industries as executive chairman but who relinquished the CEO position, was kind enough to listen to me as I coped with the transition. After the end of one particularly emotional and cathartic discussion, he looked me straight in the eye and said simply: "Phil, you've got to give up the girl."

He was right. Leaving on the right note, with as much dignity and grace as I could summon, was one of the most excruciating challenges of my career.

Key Points

- Executive directors approaching retirement age should actively engage in succession planning.

- The reality of stepping down from a position of power and authority creates a complex mix of emotions, and the difficulty should not be underestimated.

- Institutional memory is an important resource. CEOs who step down can continue to add value on a consulting or limited-partner basis.

Epilogue

I hope you get something out of this book—it's funny, I did. As I wrote, revised, and reviewed each chapter, I relived the past forty years at The Children's Aid Society, experiencing anew the exhilaration and angst of leadership. I also remembered the people who made my work so rewarding and memorable: Victor Remer, the former executive director who hired me, our board, our staff, and so many of our clients. My expertise, such as it is, is based on what I have learned from working with these wonderful people. I appreciate the opportunity to remain with Children's Aid as an adviser and am thrilled and tickled that the board has chosen to rededicate our Greenwich Village community center in my name.

However, I didn't write this book to pat myself or

my colleagues on the back—even if I do spill a lot of ink describing our work. I wrote it for you, the reader, someone involved in the day-to-day leadership of a not-for-profit organization. If you've made it through to this epilogue, I'd like to thank you for taking time from your hectic schedule to consider my advice. My most sincere hope is that my thoughts will remain with you after you close these final pages, offering new and useful insights on how to build the best possible not-for-profit organization. My goal is not to promote excellence in and of itself but to help all of us make a difference, not only in the daily lives of the children, families, and individuals we serve but also the society that surrounds us.

Further Resources

For more information on topics covered in this book, you might refer to the following:

Benioff, Marc, and Southwick, Karen. *Compassionate Capitalism—How Corporations Can Make Doing Good an Integral Part of Doing Well.* Franklin Lakes: Career Press, 2004.

Blanchard, Ken, and Waghorn, Terry. *Mission Possible. Becoming a World-Class Organization While There's Still Time.* New York: McGraw-Hill, 1997.

Brudney, Jeffrey L. "Designing and Managing Volunteer Programs." *The Jossey-Bass Handbook of Nonprofit Leadership & Management, Second Edition* (San Francisco: Robert D. Herman & Associates, 2005), 310.

Bryson, John M. "The Strategy Change Cycle."

The Jossey-Bass Handbook of Nonprofit Leadership &

Management, Second Edition (San Francisco:

Robert D. Herman & Associates, 2005), 171.

Cancelli, Anthony, Fordham University Graduate

School of Education; and Brickman, Ellen; Sanchez,

Arturo; Rivera, Glenda, Fordham University

Graduate School of Social Service. *The Children's Aid*

Society/Board of Education Community Schools:

Third Year Evaluation Report. New York: 1999.

Carrera, Michael A. *Lessons for Lifeguards: Working*

With Teens When the Topic Is Hope. New York:

Donkey Press, 1999.

Collins, Jim. *Good to Great—Why Some Companies*

Make the Leap... and Others Don't.

New York: HarperCollins, 2001.

Collins, Jim. *Good to Great and the Social Sectors.*
Boulder: 2005.

Dryfoos, Joy G., Quinn, Jane, and Barkin, Carol, eds.
Community Schools in Action. Lessons from a Decade of
Practice. New York: Oxford University Press, 2005.

Harman, Sidney. *Mind Your Own Business—*
A Maverick's Guide to Business, Leadership and Life.
New York: Doubleday, 2003.

Herman, Robert D., and Heimovics, Dick.
"Executive Leadership." *The Jossey-Bass Handbook of*
Nonprofit Leadership & Management, Second Edition
(Robert D. Herman & Associates, 2005), 153.

Hutchinson, Mary. *The 21 Best Ways to Raise Less*
Money. IPLS Press, 2004.

Jeavons, Thomas H. "Ethical Nonprofit
Management." *The Jossey-Bass Handbook of Nonprofit
Leadership & Management, Second Edition*
(Robert D. Herman & Associates, 2005) 204.

Krenichyn, Kira, Clark, Heléne; Schaefer-McDaniel,
Nicole; and Benitez, Lymari. ActKnowledge
Research, Inc. *21st Century Community Learning
Centers at Six New York City Middle Schools:
Year One Report.* New York: 2006.

McCurley, Stephen. "Keeping the Community
Involved: Recruiting and Retaining Volunteers."
*The Jossey-Bass Handbook of Nonprofit Leadership &
Management, Second Edition* (San Francisco:
Robert D. Herman & Associates, 2005), 587.

Philliber, Susan; Kaye, Jackie and Herling, Scott. "The National Evaluation of The Children's Aid Society Carrera-Model Program to Prevent Teen Pregnancy." Philliber Research Associates, Accord: May, 2001.

Segal, Jerome M. "Taking Back Our Time." *Philosophy & Public Policy Quarterly*, Volume 24, Number 1/2, Winter/Spring 2004.

Smith, Steven Rathgeb. "Managing the Challenges of Government Contracts." *The Jossey-Bass Handbook of Nonprofit Leadership & Management, Second Edition* (Robert D. Herman & Associates, 2005), 371.

Smucker, Bob. "Nonprofit Lobbying." *The Jossey-Bass Handbook of Nonprofit Leadership & Management, Second Edition* (Robert D. Herman & Associates, 2005), 230.

Wittenberg, Rudolph M. *So You Want to Help People.* New York: Association Press, 1947.

Yankey, John A., and Willen, Carol K. "Strategic Alliances." *The Jossey-Bass Handbook of Nonprofit Leadership & Management, Second Edition* (Robert D. Herman & Associates, 2005), 254.

Association Executive, September/October 2004.

Where We Are Now, Public Agenda, 2003.

Across the Board, January/February 2006.

The Aspen Idea, The Aspen Institute, Winter 2004/2005.

New York Stock Exchange Magazine (NYSE), CEO Agenda, August/September 2005.

Notes